Police Officers Help Us

Aaron R. Murray

Enslow Elementary
an imprint of

Enslow Publishers, Inc.
40 Industrial Road
Box 398
Berkeley Heights, NJ 07922
USA

http://www.enslow.com

Enslow Elementary, an imprint of Enslow Publishers, Inc.
Enslow Elementary® is a registered trademark of Enslow Publishers, Inc.

Library of Congress Cataloging-in-Publication Data

Murray, Aaron R.
  Police officers help us / Aaron Murray.
     p. cm. — (All about community helpers)
  Includes index.
  Summary: "Introduces pre-readers to simple concepts about the police officers using short sentences
and repetition of words"—Provided by publisher.
  ISBN 978-0-7660-4048-9
  1. Police—Juvenile literature. I. Title.
  HV7922.M88 2013
  363.2'3—dc23
                              2011037461

Future editions:
Paperback ISBN 978-1-4644-0052-0
ePUB ISBN 978-1-4645-0959-9
PDF ISBN 978-1-4646-0959-6

Printed in the United States of America
032012 Lake Book Manufacturing, Inc., Melrose Park, IL
10 9 8 7 6 5 4 3 2 1

To Our Readers: We have done our best to make sure all Internet Addresses in this book were active
and appropriate when we went to press. However, the author and the publisher have no control over and
assume no liability for the material available on those Internet sites or on other Web sites they may link
to. Any comments or suggestions can be sent by e-mail to comments@enslow.com or to the address on
the back cover.

♻ Enslow Publishers, Inc., is committed to printing our books on recycled paper. The paper in every
book contains 10% to 30% post-consumer waste (PCW). The cover board on the outside of each book
contains 100% PCW. Our goal is to do our part to help young people and the environment too!

Photo Credits: © 2011 Photos.com, a division of Getty Images. All rights reserved, pp. 1, 8, 16;
iStockphoto.com: © Carl Ballou, p. 3 (emergency), © Charlotte Swanson, p. 19 (top), © Jim Schemel,
p. 12, © Jodi Jacobson, pp. 22–23, © swalls, p. 3 (station); Shutterstock.com: Frances L. Fruit, p. 4,
Jack Dagley Photography, pp. 20–21, Kletrl, p. 14, Robert J. Beyers II, p. 13, Steve Estvanik, p. 6;
Shutterstock.com, pp. 10–11, 18, 19 (bottom).

Cover Photo: © 2011 Photos.com, a division of Getty Images. All rights reserved.

Note to Parents and Teachers

Help pre-readers get a jumpstart on reading. These lively stories introduce simple concepts with
repetition of words and short simple sentences. Photos and illustrations fill the pages with color and
effectively enhance the text. Free Educator Guides are available for this series at www.enslow.com.
Search for the *All About Community Helpers* series name.

Contents

Words to Know

emergency   station

Police officers
make sure people
follow laws.

Police officers help in an emergency.

Police officers stop
a person who
drives too fast.

They write a ticket.

Police officers drive police cars.

Police officers can ride horses or bicycles too.

Sometimes helicopters drop off police officers.

They take police to places they cannot get to in a car.

Police officers use computers at the police station.

Computers show where the emergencies are.

Police officers work with police dogs.

Police dogs are trained to find dangerous things.

The dogs help police officers to do their job.

Police officers need to be brave. They need to be ready to protect us.

Do you want to help keep people safe? Maybe you want to be a police officer.

Read More

Bourgeois, Paulette. *Police Officers.* Tonawanda, N.Y.: Kids Can Read, 2004.

Hamilton, Kersten. *Police Officers on Patrol.* New York: Viking Juvenile, 2009.

Scarry, Huck. *A Day at the Police Station.* New York: Golden Books, 2004.

Web Sites

Davis, California, Police Department Kids Page
<http://cityofdavis.org/police/kids.cfm>

Enchanted Learning. Community Helpers.
<http://www.enchantedlearning.com/
themescommunityhelpers.shtml>

Index

Guided Reading Level: C
Guided Reading Leveling System is based on the guidelines recommended by Fountas and Pinnell.

Word Count: 117